·A·B·O·R·T·I·O·N·

Jenny Bryan

Points of View

Abortion
Advertising
Alcohol
Animal Rights
Censorship
Crime and Punishment
Divorce
Drugs

Medical Ethics
Northern Ireland
Nuclear Weapons
Racism
Sex and Sexuality
Smoking
Terrorism

Front cover: *The debate over abortion centres on the relationship of the rights of the mother, the rights of the father and the rights of an embryo or fetus.*

Series Editor: William Wharfe
Editor: Elizabeth Spiers
Designer: David Armitage

First published in 1991 by
Wayland (Publishers) Limited
61 Western Road, Hove
East Sussex BN3 1JD, England

British Library Cataloguing in Publication Data
Bryan, Jenny
      Abortion. – (Points of view)
      1. Abortion
      I. Title   II. Series
      363.46
ISBN 1-85210-655-7

Phototypeset by Direct Image Photosetting Ltd,
Hove, East Sussex, England
Printed in Italy by G. Canale & C.S.pA, Turin
Bound in France by A.G.M.

Acknowledgements

The publishers have attempted to contact all copyright holders of the quotations in this title, and apologise if there have been any oversights.
The publishers gratefully acknowledge permission from the following to reproduce extracts from copyright material: Basil Blackwell, *Bioethics*, by Mary Anne Warren, 1989, vol 4, p 320; British Medical Association, *Philosophy and Practice of Medical Ethics*, 1988; *British Medical Journal*, (1) article by Diane Munday, 1989, vol 298, p 1231; (2) chart, 1989, vol 298, p 1231–4; CIOMS, *Ethics and Human Values in Family Planning*, by Professor H. Hathout, edited by Z. Bankowski, J. Barzelatto and AM. Capron, 1989; *Daily Appelate Report*, (1) Chief Justice Rehnquist, 6 July 1989; (2) Justice John P. Stevens, 6 July 1989; *Daily Mail*, anonymous woman, 7 December 1989; *Daily Telegraph*, (1) article by Dr Alexandra Anca, 8 January 1990; (2) article by Baroness Seear, 15 December 1989; (3) article, 20 February,1990; *Ethics and Medicine*, anonymous woman, 1986, vol 2:3 p 39; *General Practitioner*, (1) Professor Etienne-Emile Beaulieu, 6 October 1989; (2) Ariel Mouttet, 6 October 1989; *Guardian*, (1) article by Lyn Thomas, 5 January 1990; (2) article by Dame Mary Donaldson, 12 December 1989; (3) article by Melanie Phillips, 1 December 1989; (4) 'Frances', 28 November 1989; (5) Louise Minter, 2 January 1989; (6) nursing sister working at an abortion clinic, 2 November 1989; HMSO, (1) *Human IVF, Embryo Research, Fetal Tissue for Research and Treatment, and Abortion: International Information*, by Jennifer Gunning, February 1990; (2) *Human Fertilization and Embryology Bill*, 1989; *Independent*, (1) Tracy Allsop, 10 April 1990; (2) Dr Tim Rutter, 7 February 1990; (3) Right Reverend Hugh Montefiore, 26 January 1987; (4) Robert Hercz, 25 February 1987; (5) Michael Bell, 25 February 1987; (6) Sir John Donaldson, 25 February 1987; (7) Professor David Baird, 15 August 1989; *Independent Magazine*, article by Randall Terry, 20 January 1990; *Journal of the American Medical Association*, (1) article by Gerard Brungardt, 1989, vol 262, p 1187; (2) J. Todd Williams, 1989, vol 262, p 1877; (3) article by Dr Judy Brown, 17 November 1989; (4) J. Todd Williams, 1989, vol 262, p 1877; (5) Diane Dahm, 1989, vol 262, p 1876; (6) and (7) J. Todd Williams, 1989, vol 262, p 1877; *Journal of Medical Ethics*, (1) anonymous mother of handicapped child, 1983, vol 9, p 152; (2) article by Richard Lilford and Nicholas Johnson, 1989, vol 15, p 82; King Edward's Hospital Fund for London, *Rights and Wrongs in Medicine*, by Sir Immanuel Jakobovits, edited by Peter Byrne, 1986; *Lancet*, (1) article, *Reagan's Revenge*, 1989, vol 2, p 116; (2) and (3) article, *Abortion Ruling in Quebec*, by Diana Brahams, 1989, vol 2, p 340; (4) article by Dr R.J. Wapner *et al*, 1990, vol 1, p 90; (5) article, *Gynaecologists' Attitudes to Abortion*, by Wendy Savage and Colin Francome, 1989, vol 2, p 1323; (6) article, *Late Abortions*, by D.P. Paintin, 1989, vol 2, p 563; London and International Publishers, (1) *Abortion in Demand*, by Victoria Greenwood and Jock Young, 1976; (2) *Society and Fertility*, by Malclom Potts and Peter Shelman, 1979; Martin Secker and Warburg, *Sex and Destiny – the Politics of Human Fertility*, by Germaine Greer, 1984; *New Scientist*, article by Dr Anne McLaren, 24 April 1986; *New Statesman and Society*, (1) Claude Evin, 29 September 1989; (2) Phyllis Bowman, 29 September 1989; *News of the World*, Peter Marshall, 31 December 1989; Oxford University Press, *Moral Dilemmas in Modern Medicine*, edited by Michael Lockwood, 1985; *Sunday Express*, article by Johanna Kaufmann, 12 November 1989; *Sunday Times*, article by Rabbi Julia Neuberger, 1 March 1987; *The Times*, (1) Mary Sue Davis, 10 August 1989; (2) Junior 'JR' Davis, 10 August 1989; (3) Sir Bernard Braine, 3 April 1990; (4) Brian Rix *et al*, 4 June 1985; (5) Sir Bernard Braine, 3 April 1990; Unwin Hyman Ltd, *Test Tube Women*, edited by R. Arditti, R, Klein and S. Minden, (1) article by Barbara Katz Rothman; (2) and (3) article by K. Kaufmann, 1984.

Contents

Introduction

'Please don't kill me, Mummy!' scream the placards. Women turning up at many abortion clinics in the USA and the UK are today having to cope with more than the feelings of fear, sadness and guilt that are likely to go with the decision to terminate a pregnancy. They now have to face the anger and hatred of anti-abortion campaigners – many of them members of Operation Rescue – who picket clinics and try to dissuade them from going through with their abortions.

> I saw about eight to 10 people with arms linked, so that there were no gaps, just barricading the door in a triangle formation, and a lot of other people milling around.

> People that were trying to come in were being pulled down the drive and they were shouting 'leave me alone.'

> The demonstrators were shouting 'don't go in, they will kill your baby.' (Tracy Allsopp, Abortion Clinic Manager, *Independent*, 10 April 1990.)

Anti-abortionists picket a US clinic in an attempt to stop women from having their pregnancies terminated.

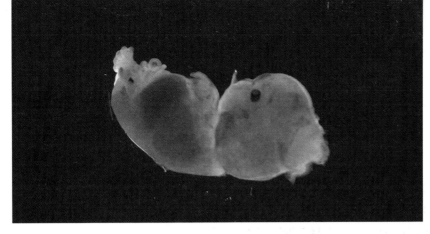

A human fetus at about six weeks' gestation, when the mother may not even be sure that she is pregnant. However, the fetus has begun to grow limbs, and some internal organs have developed.

To anti-abortionists, a person is alive from the moment a human egg is fertilized, and any attempt to end that life — at any stage before or after birth — is murder.

> If you were sitting at home and you could hear the screams of four and five year olds being molested or killed, would you write your Congressman or go and rescue those innocent children? There's no difference between killing a four-year-old child and aborting a pre-born, three month old child. It's no less murder because the child cannot scream. (Randall Terry, Founder of Operation Rescue, USA, *Independent Magazine, 20 January 1990.*)

It is hard to see how there can ever be a compromise between people who hold views like this and those who believe that abortion should be available to all women, on demand.

> Choice and information have served as the cornerstones of the women's health and the reproductive rights movements. We are, above all, pro-choice. We support the rights of the individual woman to choose, to choose pregnancy or abortion, to choose alternative medical treatments or none at all. (Barbara Katz Rothman, *Test Tube Women*, 1984.)

Somewhere, in the middle ground, are those who believe that abortion should be available, but only for specific medical or social reasons: women for whom an unwanted child would be a catastrophe both for themselves, their family and their baby; women who have been raped; women who know that their fetuses are handicapped; women for whom pregnancy or childbirth would be medically dangerous; women who simply could not cope with the demands of caring for a child.

But how is society to decide where the boundaries should lie? Is it a matter simply for the law-makers, the politicians, the medical profession and the spiritual leaders? Or is it something that each one of us should decide for ourselves?

What the law says

> You cannot legislate against abortion. The people who would like to do so are up against the human, practical problem that a woman who does not want her baby cannot be compelled to give birth. Nothing could show more clearly than the Romanian experience, that even draconian [very severe] legislation does not succeed. We have to understand that, and the pro-lifers have to accept it. If women are sufficiently determined not to bear a child to term, they will always find ways of getting rid of it. It was ever thus, throughout history. (Dr Tim Rutter, consultant to Marie Stopes International, *Independent*, 7 February 1990.)

Is he right?

Under the Ceaușescu regime in Romania, to which Dr Rutter refers, abortion was illegal and women were told they must have at least five children. It is only since the dictator's overthrow and execution in December 1989 that the effect of such a policy has become apparent:

> Unfortunately, our wards still contain many victims of the dictator's lunatic restrictions, which we as doctors were forced to carry through although virtually none of us agreed with them. Many thousands of those forced to backstreet abortions suffered sterility. The unluckiest died. (Dr Alexandru Anca, senior Romanian gynaecologist, *Daily Telegraph*, 8 January 1990)

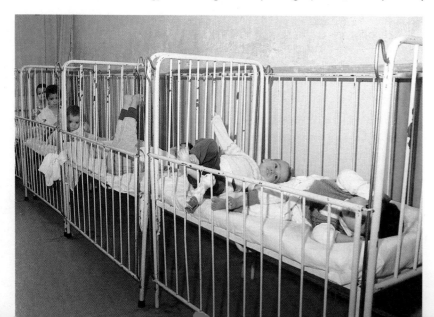

Romanian children, abandoned by their parents because they could not care for them, wait for someone to claim or adopt them.

A one-room slum in Shoreditch, East London, in 1919, showing the desperate conditions in which whole families lived before contraception and abortion made it easier for couples to plan their families according to their ability to look after them.

In the UK, the 1967 Abortion Act was introduced largely to prevent just this kind of terrible toll that so-called 'backstreet', or illegal, abortion was taking on women's health. By legalizing the operation, politicians hoped that fewer women would die or suffer permanent damage as a result of badly performed abortions. It seems they were right:

> The number of women discharged from hospital with a diagnosis of sepsis caused by an abortion was 3050 in 1965. By 1975 this figure had fallen to 710 and was down to 390 in 1982. In 1989 most young doctors who were trained in Britain have never seen a woman suffering or dying from the effects of criminal abortion. (Diane Munday, *British Medical Journal*, 1989, vol 298, p 1231.)

Today, abortion is illegal in remarkably few countries – even those with strong religious traditions. During the 1960s and 1970s, many governments, like that in the UK, relaxed their abortion laws and made it easier for women to terminate unwanted pregnancies. But, in recent years, some have begun to rethink their policies.

In 1980, the US Supreme Court undermined a previous decision that abortion should be the constitutional right of all American women by barring public employees from performing or assisting in abortions not being carried out for medical reasons:

> Nothing in the Constitution requires the State to enter or remain in the abortion business or entitles private physicians and their patients to access to public facilities for the performance of abortions. (Chief Justice Rehnquist, *Daily Appellate Report*, 6 July 1989.)

Justice Harry Blackmun, who was one of those responsible for the Roe v Wade decision that shaped the USA abortion laws from 1973 to 1989 and gave women the right to abortion, commented:

> I fear for the future, for the freedom and equality of millions of women. (*Lancet*, 1989, vol 2, p 116.)

Although each state continues to make its own ruling on abortion, these measures will, in effect, make it very much harder for poor

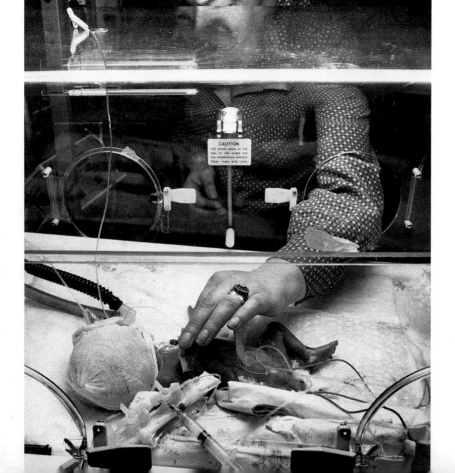

It hardly seems possible that this little girl, born at 26 weeks and weighing just 850 g, could have survived. Thanks to modern technology, she has. Fetuses of this age can be legally aborted in some countries.

American women to get an abortion. It will be available only in expensive private clinics. In Idaho, for example, abortion is now legal only in certain cases of rape and incest, if the fetus is 'profoundly' deformed or if the pregnancy threatens the mother's life.

Many of the recent attempts to change abortion laws have centred on efforts to reduce the time limit at which abortion can occur. However, this has only happened in the UK. Here, the time limit for abortion after the 1967 Abortion Bill was 28 weeks, because it was assumed that no baby could survive outside the womb before that time. Now, thanks to medical advances, babies born at 25 weeks frequently survive. There have also been a few cases in which babies born at 24 weeks have survived.

In 1989, Lord Houghton introduced a Bill aimed at reducing the already small number of late abortions.

> We are not saying [legal] abortion is desirable. We are saying it is the lesser of two evils. The evidence now is that it is sensible to reduce the upper limit to 24 weeks. If we do not do this now, the issue will return again and again. It will not go away. We have a reasonable proposition here, overwhelmingly supported by the best medical evidence that can be produced. (Baroness Seear, *Daily Telegraph*, 15 December 1989.)

In April 1990, the time limit was reduced to 24 weeks, except in cases of serious fetal abnormality or danger to the mother, where no limit has been set. However, this has yet to be finalized. However, the anti-abortion groups have dismissed this as a:

> barefaced measure to allow unborn children to be killed up to birth on social grounds. (*Daily Telegraph*, 20 February 1990.)

Ironically, despite the anti-abortion policy of the former Romanian government, it is in some communist countries that abortion laws are most lax; indeed, in the Soviet Union, a country where the Pill is not available and condoms are in very short supply, abortion is seen simply as an alternative to contraception.

> In the western part of the Soviet Union it is not unusual for a woman to have eight or nine abortions in a lifetime. Demand for contraception is unbelievable. At the moment, abortion is one of the most widely used methods. (Lyn Thomas, acting European Director of the International Planned Parenthood Federation, *Guardian*, 5 January 1990.)

Rates of legal abortion per thousand women aged 15-44 in the most recent available year.

Country	Year	Rate of abortion per 1000 women aged 15-44
Netherlands	1984	5.6
Scotland	1984	8.9
New Zealand	1984	9.7
England & Wales	1984	12.8
Canada	1984	13.0
Norway	1984	15.9
Sweden	1984	17.7
Denmark	1984	18.4
German Democratic Republic	1984	26.6
United States	1983	27.4
Hungary	1984	37.1
Cuba	1984	58.6
China	1983	61.5
Yugoslavia	1984	70.3
USSR	1982	181.0

(*British Medical Journal*, 1989, vol 298, p 1231-4.)

International time limits on abortion

Country	Indication	Time limit
UK	Risk to life of woman or her mental or physical health Substantial risk of handicap in child	Viability of fetus (ie: 28 weeks [now reduced to 24 weeks])
Australia	Physical and mental health of woman, fetal defect, rape	14-28 weeks (dep on State)
Denmark	On request Medical, genetic, rape or social with permission of committee	12 weeks 2nd trimester (up to the 6th month)
Italy	On demand Medical or genetic reasons or rape	Up to 90 days No limit
Spain	Rape Genetic reasons Medical reasons	12 weeks 22 weeks No limit
USA	5 states make abortion illegal Other states, e.g. California and Virginia, have liberal laws Many states prohibit public funding of abortion	

Queueing is a way of life for Russians in a country where many commodities are in short supply — from fresh fruit and vegetables to condoms.

(*Human IVF, embryo research, fetal tissue for research and treatment and abortion: International information,* Jennifer Gunning, February 1990, HMSO.)

In China – another communist country – there is evidence that women are forced to have abortions rather than disobey the government's one-child-per-family policy, aimed at reducing the country's massive overpopulation problems.

> . . . the Beijing government is intensifying its birth control efforts [including] the use of pay/promotion/termination as inducements or threats to participation, the cutting off of water and electricity to those who do not comply, and the use of forced sterilization and abortion . . . The policies and procedures of the Chinese government run counter to [against] the heritage of the practice of medicine. (Gerard Brungardt, *Journal of the American Medical Association*, 1989, vol 262, p 1187.)

The very fact that so many attempts have been made to change the abortion laws of different countries suggests that no government has yet managed to balance the rights of the mother, father and child to the satisfaction of all its voters.

1 Should governments be able to legislate on abortion, or should it be left to each couple to decide whether or not to give birth to the child they have conceived?

2 Look at the laws in the table and consider which you would agree with most.

3 Imagine you are a law-maker and devise what you think would be a fair set of rules, governing when and under what circumstances you think abortion should be allowed.

In China, couples are offered financial incentives to limit their families to one child. In some areas, great pressure is put on women to have subsequent pregnancies terminated.

3

The role of religion

No religion actively supports abortion. But some religions are more prepared than others to accept that there are situations where abortion may be necessary. On the one hand, the Vatican has made it very clear where the Roman Catholic Church stands on the subject:

> The direct interruption of the generative process already begun, and, above all, directly willed and procured abortion, even if for therapeutic reasons, are to be absolutely excluded as licit [lawful] means of regulating birth. (Papal encyclical, *Humanae Vitae*, 1968.)

Pope John Paul II has continued to emphasize the anti-abortion stance of the Roman Catholic church.

The Archbishop of Canterbury, Dr George Carey. The Anglican church has tended to take a more liberal view towards abortion.

But the stance of many representatives of the Church of England is less clear-cut. In 1985, for example, the Bishop of Birmingham put up a Bill in the House of Lords proposing that the time limit for abortion in the UK should be reduced to 24 weeks:

> I am not an absolutist. I recognize that there are situations where abortion is right. People say that only 33 babies over 24 weeks' gestation were aborted in 1985, but the numbers are not relevant. I am very surprised that anyone should think that 33 babies were not worth saving. (Right Reverend Hugh Montefiore, *Independent*, 26 January 1987.)

Contrast this relatively liberal attitude of a leading British churchman with that of Belgium's deeply religious head of state, King Baudouin, who, in 1990, briefly relinquished the throne rather than put his signature to a Bill legalizing abortion.

Much of the discussion centres around the point at which life begins. In Jewish law, life starts only at the moment of birth. In the early part of the Talmud, it is defined as the moment when either the head or the greater part of the child emerges from the birth canal. However, in practice, abortion is discouraged, except in life-threatening circumstances:

> . . . while we attach a very precious value to the unborn child and would only under the most exceptional circumstances be entitled to terminate a pregnancy, it is nevertheless regarded as a potential human being only, and therefore, in the event for instance of any mortal conflict between mother and child before birth, where a continued pregnancy might cause a risk of life to the mother, we would have no hesitation, no qualms of any kind, not only in sanctioning the destruction of her unborn child in order to save the mother, but in requiring it, making it mandatory to destroy this unborn life in order to save the existing life of the mother. (Sir Immanuel Jakobovits, Chief Rabbi, *Rights and Wrongs in Medicine*, edited by Peter Byrne, 1986.)

Jewish people at the Wailing Wall in Israel. The Jewish faith discourages abortion, except when the life of the mother is at risk.

Muslim teaching states that abortion is wrong and can be justified only in very rare circumstances, such as when the mother's life is in danger.

Muslims hold a similar view, and abortion is rarely sanctioned:

> A woman does not create the fetus but receives it; the fetus is entrusted to her . . . Woman's freedom with regard to her body cannot entail the freedom to kill 'another' human being, merely because it is inside her . . .
>
> Only when the mother has a disease that makes the continuation of pregnancy a threat to her life is abortion permitted. In this case, the mother juridically [in a court of law] is considered the root and the fetus the offshoot, and the offshoot may be sacrificed to save the root. (Professor H. Hathout, *Ethics and Human Values in Family Planning*, edited by Z. Bankowski, J. Barzelatto and A. M. Capron, 1989, Council for International Medical Organizations of Medical Sciences (CIOMS), WHO, Geneva.)

1   Do you follow any particular religion? If so, what do you know of the teachings about abortion of your religion? Do you agree with them?

2   Do you agree with the Jewish and Muslim faiths that the mother's life should come before that of her unborn child? Explain your answer.

3   How well qualified are religious leaders to guide their followers about the rights and wrongs of abortion?

But do religious leaders have a monopoly on moral thinking? Cannot some of our leading philosophers also give us some insights into the rights and wrongs of abortion? One view, for example, holds that life as we know it begins only when the brain is formed:

> Just as I shall live only as long as the relevant part of my brain remains essentially intact, so I came into existence only when the appropriate part or parts of my brain came into existence, or more precisely, reached the appropriate stage of development to sustain my identity as a human being with the capacity for consciousness . . .
>
> Presumably, then, my life began somewhere between conception and birth. Certainly not at conception, and certainly not before my brain came into being . . . (*Moral Dilemmas in Modern Medicine*, edited by Michael Lockwood, 1985.)

The same author therefore argues:

> There is all the difference in the world between killing a week old embryo and killing a neonate [newborn]. Neither may be a person. But the second is a human being, with an interest in continued life. When all that exists is the embryo, on the other hand, there is nothing there to have interests. You and I were new-born infants; we were never week-old embryos, any more than we were sperm or ova or (except metaphorically) twinkles in our parents' eyes. (*Moral Dilemmas in Modern Medicine*, edited by Michael Lockwood, 1985.)

But the moral rights and wrongs of abortion cannot be seen in isolation. There are many other medical and social factors that need to be considered and may, perhaps, take precedence over any discussion of when and how a life begins.

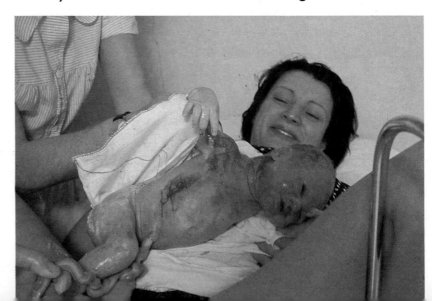

The moment of joy at the birth of a much-wanted child. But should an embryo only a few weeks after conception have the same rights as a full-term, newborn baby?

16

4

The rights of the mother

By this stage in a pregnancy a woman will be very much aware of her baby kicking and moving in her womb. But throughout her pregnancy, the rights of the mother take precedence, in most countries, over those of her fetus.

In countries that allow abortion, the mother's needs are inevitably put before those of her fetus. It may be agreed that she is unable, by reason of age, health, mental development or social deprivation, to care for her child and so she has an abortion.

> It is, I think, a feature of our ordinary moral thinking . . . that there is a limit to the degree of self sacrifice that can reasonably be demanded of someone in the name of duty. Perhaps it is just too much to ask of a woman that she be made to endure the trauma of birth and the burden of pregnancy against her will, especially if there are contributory circumstances, such as extreme youth or rape, that make the whole business even more of an ordeal. (*Moral Dilemmas in Modern Medicine*, edited by Michael Lockwood, 1985.)

But anti-abortion groups argue that abortion is psychologically damaging to the woman, since it goes against her every instinct:

> Motherhood is ordained [destined] to nurture and to protect. Its instinct is normally self-sacrificial. The hardest thing of all to bear, harder than the loss of the child itself, is the fact of having deliberately surrendered your own child to death. Many women suffer agonies after a miscarriage, feeling that they failed their child and that their bodies betrayed them and their maternity.
>
> It is very hard then to imagine what it is like for a woman who has had an abortion to face the fact there really was a child, she really was a mother. (Anonymous woman who regretted her own abortion, *Ethics and Medicine*, 1986, vol 2:3, p39.)

But what of those young, single women for whom the idea of an unwanted child is devastating? What do they think? A series of women gave their views in a recent survey:

> I come from Ireland and I know for a fact that if people faced reality there, they would see so many young people ruining their lives by being pushed into marriage because they are pregnant and ruining their lives, their husband's and their babies. They think that by having no clinics like these that young girls will be afraid to get pregnant and won't have intercourse, which is rubbish! There is so many children battered and beaten because their parents cannot stand the pressures and are too young to be able to cope with life! (21-year-old woman, *Abortion in Practice in Britain and the US*, by Colin Francome, 1986.)

A new baby can bring joy to one woman, but heartache to another if she feels unable to care for him or her. An unwanted child puts great pressure on a couple's relationship.

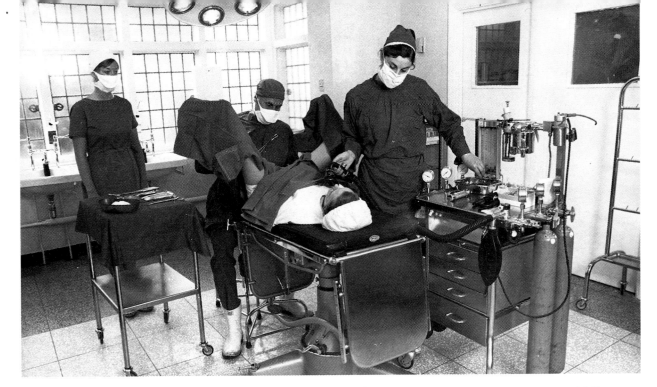

The doctors' examinations are over and the forms have been signed. Twenty minutes or so in the operating theatre and it will all be over. But the woman may bear emotional scars of her decision long after the physical ones have healed.

> Even though I have been through an abortion I would like others not to use abortion as another form of contraceptive. For abortion is not preventing a birth but killing an individual . . . Abortion is a serious matter and should be treated so, especially by those terminating a baby.
>
> Even though I have had an abortion, I hope and pray I never have to go through it again for moral and emotional reasons. (17-year-old single Catholic girl, *Abortion in Practice in Britain and the US*, by Colin Francome, 1986.)

Perhaps we should be doing more, though, to spare such women the need to have abortions by providing them with the economic and social support they need to help bring up their babies. That way, they could have a real choice whether or not to have their child:

> Abortion out of economic necessity is a tragedy. It must be demanded from government not as a dispensation to women but as a consequence of the government's own failure to provide facilities for children and support for the mother. Abortion out of choice, where no overriding economic pressures occur, is a fundamental right of women to control their own fertility, it is a comment on the inadequacy of contraceptive technology and a pre-requisite for women's social equality. (*Abortion in Demand*, by Victoria Greenwood and Jock Young, 1976.)

This mother-of-ten finds it very hard to manage, and her children are growing up disadvantaged. Will they be locked into the same cycle of unwanted pregnancies and poverty?

However, some people believe that we are too quick to hide behind the social and economic arguments in favour of abortion and that, in reality, the vast majority of abortions owe little to such considerations:

> Does the circumstance of birth, whether a child is conceived by an impoverished mother or a PhD candidate, merit its disposal into the suction chamber? None of us could dictate our conception.

While it is true that many children are born into less than desirable conditions, the vast majority, regardless of social, economic or racial status, are resoundingly thankful that the opportunity to live was granted them. We hide behind the guise of situational ethics, arguing incessantly about rape victims, anencephalic [absence of part or all of the brain] gestations, and the dangers to maternal life, while we neglect to face the reality that the majority of all abortions are of the convenience or 'alternative birth control' variety. (J. Todd Williams, *Journal of the American Medical Association*, 1989, vol 262, p 1877.)

Some would argue that a change in the abortion laws should take more account of the reasons for an abortion. For example, cases where the fetus is seriously damaged or the mother's life is somehow threatened would be looked on more favourably than those where requests for abortion were made for the following type of reason:

> I was a single woman; I had no 'steady boyfriend' or 'lover'. Both pregnancies were the result of short, casual sexual relationships and irresponsible attitudes, theirs and mine, towards birth control. Under the circumstances there was never the least thought of having a baby, either as a couple or as a single parent.

I received the result of the pregnancy test and made the appointment for the abortion with the same phone call . . . (K. Kaufmann, *Test Tube Women*, 1984.)

Does this woman, for example, deserve the same availability of abortion services as the woman below:

> 'I'm glad you called. There's a problem.' For the rest of my life, I will remember those words. I was in the 12th week of my

When abortions are carried out	
Country	Up to week 13
USA	91%
Britain	86%
Sweden	95%
Denmark	97%

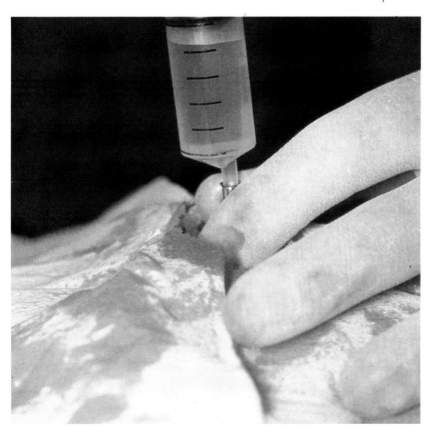

A sample of the fluid that surrounds the fetus is taken for analysis. The woman will be offered a termination of her pregnancy if any abnormality is found.

21

> pregnancy and had just finished a routine obstetric visit . . . Five minutes later I was back in my doctor's office, saying words beyond comprehension: 'The chromosomes are not normal'.

. . . Should we let nature take its course? Perhaps we had no right to consider ending the pregnancy . . .

One week later, we went to hospital to end the pregnancy. My husband was very supportive, but I was the one to walk into the operating room alone. It took several weeks to recover physically; emotional scars are still raw 2 years later. (Dr Judy Brown, *Journal of the American Medical Association*, 17 November 1989.)

But, if we deny an abortion to the first woman, who will suffer? She or the child she does not want? Or should more time have been spent discussing the alternatives with her?

> I genuinely empathize with the woman carrying the unplanned child. Too often she has been relegated to the handouts at abortion clinics or to advice by biased physicians.

Though in many cases her heart tells her otherwise, she finds no support and destroys her baby.

Should we not instead nurture responsibility and emphasize alternatives such as adoption? Indeed, adoption agencies are overrun with hopeful couples, but the supply of babies is limited. (J. Todd Williams, *Journal of the American Medical Association*, 1989, vol 262, p 1877.)

Has the pendulum swung too far, then, towards the needs of the woman who wants an abortion and forgotten those of her partner, her fetus and, not least, of society?

1   Should it be easier for some women: e.g. the poor, single parents or mothers-to-be with social/housing problems, to get an abortion than others, or do you agree with J. Todd Williams (see quotation above right) that these reasons are used too often as an excuse for irresponsible behaviour?

2   In industrialized countries, there is a huge shortage of healthy babies for adoption by infertile couples. Do you think more women who want an abortion should be encouraged to give birth and give their children up for abortion?

3   If a country allows abortion, who should pay for the operation: the state or the pregnant woman?

What happens in an abortion

Up to week 16: the fetus is sucked out of the womb by vacuum aspiration. The cervical canal that leads into the womb is stretched open and a tube passed through so that the fetus and placenta can be removed. This is normally done under general anaesthetic and takes about 10 minutes. In some cases, this method is used up to 20 weeks.

After week 16: labour is induced with drugs so that the woman gives birth to the fetus. This is because to stretch the cervix artificially to the size needed to remove the fetus could cause permanent damage. The drugs that are used set in motion the dilatation of the cervix and contractions that occur during a normal birth. The woman is therefore conscious, but heavily sedated, throughout and the procedure can take several hours. The baby is born whole but is usually dead. In the case of a very late abortion − after 22 weeks − it is possible that the child will show signs of life for a few minutes.

5

The rights of the father

In the last few years, a number of men, in countries as far apart as Norway, the UK and Canada, have gone to the courts to try to prevent their partners from having abortions. All have ultimately failed.

> As the law stands we have no rights. Our babies can be killed and I'm told we can't arrange decent burial. We can't even prevent the foetus being used for medical experiments. (Peter Marshall, father of child aborted against his wishes, *News of the World*, 31 December 1989.)

Is this fair? Genetically, the fetus is as much a part of its father as of its mother. So should they not have equal rights in deciding whether it should live?

This young father plays an important part in the upbringing of his son. Perhaps he should also have some say in a decision about aborting any future children.

23

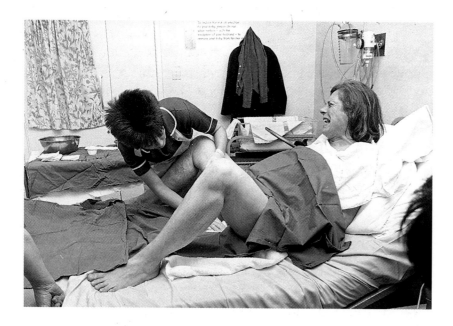

It is the woman who bears the pain of delivery, so how can any decision about abortion be left to her partner?

In the much-publicized words of Robert Hercz, the Norwegian man who tried to prevent his girlfriend having an abortion:

> All you've got to do is go through the pregnancy and birth. (*Independent*, 25 February 1987.)

How do you think a woman would feel if someone said that?

In 1987, in the UK, a university student tried to prevent his girlfriend from aborting their fetus under a 60-year-old British law that says a fetus cannot be aborted if it is capable of being born alive. The fetus in this case was between 18 and 21 weeks old.

> Even if a child is only capable of showing signs of life for a very short time it is still capable of being born alive and so is again protected by the Act . . . A child at 21 weeks is capable of being born alive. I have well authenticated cases of children of 22 weeks gestation surviving. If that is so then sooner or later a child of 21 weeks will survive.
>
> It is a moral absurdity that a child has no protection in the law at one stage of gestation and a few minutes later has got protection. (Michael Bell, Lawyers for the Defence of the Unborn, *Independent*, 25 February 1987.)

But the judges in the case disagreed:

> A fetus which is so far undeveloped that any separation from the mother would mean it cannot breathe naturally or with the help of a ventilator is not a child capable of being born alive . . . (Sir John Donaldson, Master of the Rolls, Court of Appeal, *Independent*, 25 February 1987.)

Two years later, a Canadian man whose partner was 21 weeks pregnant with his fetus did win two rounds of the legal battle to prevent it from being aborted. In upholding the injunction banning the woman from having an abortion, Mr Justice Yves Bernier commented:

> Pregnancy is not in itself an attack on a woman's physical well-being or an interference in her body, but a function which is a fundamental part of her nature. The rule of nature is that pregnancy must lead to birth . . . The right to the voluntary interruption of pregnancy is one allowed under certain exceptions. (*Lancet*, 1989, vol 2, p 340.)

He decided that the pregnancy was too advanced to merit such an exception and added that to allow an abortion in this case:

> would be a denial of all legal interests of the father who, as much as the mother, was the author of the conception. It would also mean considering the child which has been conceived but not yet born as a non-being. (*Lancet*, 1989, vol 2, p 340.)

Rabbi Julia Neuberger, who has argued forcefully that the rights of the father in any decision about aborting his child should depend on the nature of his relationship with his partner.

What is a test-tube baby?

The scientific name for this technique is *in vitro* fertilization. The woman is given hormones to make her produce several eggs, which are removed from her ovaries and mixed, in the laboratory, with sperm from her partner. The fertilized eggs are then replaced in her womb and, hopefully, develop into one or more babies.

Sometimes, embryos are frozen and stored so that the couple can have further attempts at having a baby. This may mean that babies 'conceived' at the same time may be born several years apart.

Nevertheless, the woman fled to the USA and had the abortion there. So it seems that, even when the law is on the man's side, it is impossible, as pointed out in chapter 2, to make a woman give birth to a child if she does not want to.

In the Canadian case, the verdict of Justice Bernier and his colleagues was subsequently overturned – after the abortion had taken place.

Perhaps future decisions should take account of the nature of the relationship between the parents of the fetus:

> A man who makes a permanent commitment to a woman presumably in marriage or arguably in a long-term 'common law' union has a clear stake in the lives of their shared children.
>
> He also has a say in whether they should commence life – over contraception and, in some cases, abortion. That cannot be as great as the mother's, but the father, by virtue of his relationship with the mother and their mutual children, is an influential factor.
>
> If, however, a man does not make that commitment he cannot have any status in the debate. (Rabbi Julia Neuberger, *Sunday Times*, 1 March 1987.)

Another aspect of the debate centres on the rights of parents to embryos conceived in the laboratory – so-called test-tube babies. These embryos can be frozen for long periods, but what if the parents separate before the embryos are implanted in their mother's womb?

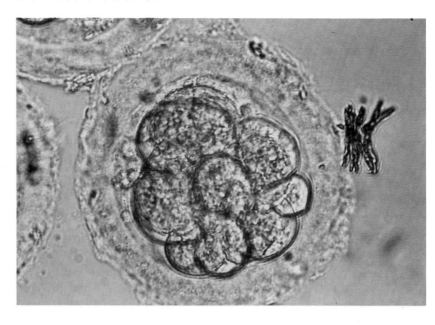

Just a clump of cells in the laboratory. But these particular cells were to become the world's first 'ice baby' twins – conceived in the laboratory, frozen, thawed and later replaced in their mother's womb.

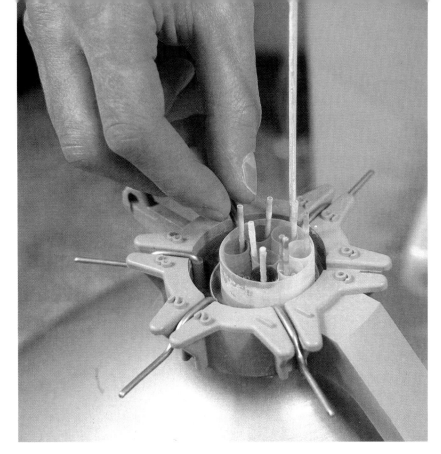

Each of these straws contains frozen embryos, which will be stored for their parents until they are ready to try for a baby.

In 1989, an American couple fought over custody of seven such embryos:

> I am the mother of the embryos. I consider them my children. The only person who has a right to them is me. (Mary Sue Davis, *The Times*, 10 August 1989.)

But her husband, who wanted the embryos destroyed, argued:

> There is no way I want to put a child of mine in a single-parent home. (Mr Junior 'JR' Davis, *The Times*, 10 August 1989.)

The result has been a protracted legal battle that could take years to decide.

The British Government, in an attempt to clarify the situation concerning possession of frozen embryos, inserted a clause in the 1989 Human Fertilization and Embryology Bill:

> An embryo, the creation of which is brought about *in vitro* [in the test tube] must not be kept in storage unless there is an effective consent, by each person whose gametes [sex cells] were used to bring about the creation of the embryo, to the storage of the embryo and the embryo is stored in accordance with those consents.

But who would envy the first lawyer who tries to test the law on behalf of a client wishing to withdraw that consent?

---

1 How much say do you think the father should have in whether or not his unborn child is aborted?

2 If a man can prove that he can provide a stable home to bring up his child, should he be able to insist that his partner gives birth to the baby and hands it over to him?

3 Who do you think should have the rights to frozen embryos if a couple divorce, or do you think the embryos should be destroyed?

27

6

Rights before birth

When does the fetus take on rights of its own? Never has this question been more relevant. Major advances in medicines over the last decade have left us not only with the ethical dilemma of abortion, but also of whether embryos can be used for research before they are destroyed. Those in favour of such research stress the difference in timescale; many countries allow abortion up to 24 or 28 weeks of pregnancy, but 14 days is becoming the accepted limit for embryo research.

> Abortion law reform and embryo research are two separate issues. How can one logically relate the abortion of a fetus, a recognisable human being, with the destruction, in the cause of responsible, worthwhile research, of the fertilized egg, at implantation the size of a full stop? (Dame Mary Donaldson, *Guardian*, 12 December 1989.)

Below *A diagram to show four stages of fetal development: (1) at 8 weeks; (2) at 16 weeks; (3) at 28 weeks and (4) just before birth, at 40 weeks. Should a fetus have rights at any, or all, of these stages?*

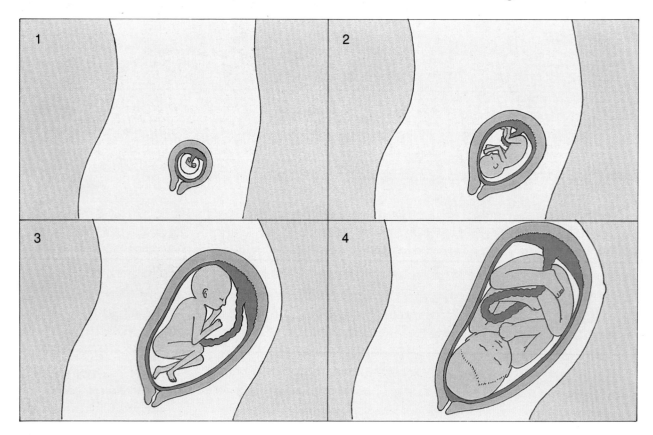

An anti-abortion demonstration. To these people, abortion for any reason, and at any stage after conception, is murder.

Yet, to the anti-abortion groups, as we have already seen, an embryo has the same rights at egg fertilization – when it is just two cells old – as the day it is a newborn child.

> The question posed . . . is a very simple one. Do we favour the destruction of human life or not? (Sir Bernard Braine, *The Times*, 3 April 1990.)

Live embryos have only become available for research with the advent of *in vitro* fertilization – and the birth of test-tube babies to previously infertile couples. Sometimes, there are 'spare embryos' that are not needed and it is these that have been used to try to find out more about serious, sometimes inherited, diseases.

> In my view, if a pre-embryo or even an unfertilised egg is intended for transfer to a uterus, to develop into a wanted child, then it is entitled to all the protection that we can give it, and should never be used for research that might in any way prejudice its chances of giving rise to a normal baby. That entitlement is because of what it is going to be, not because of what it is. For most people, a pre-embryo is not a person or a human being or an unborn child, and we do not expend grief or ceremony over the thousands lost with the menstrual flow every month. So if a pre-embryo is not intended to be transferred to a uterus, in other words if it has no future, then it seems to me positively good that it should be used for research . . . Of course such research should be properly regulated and licensed. (Dr Ann McLaren, *New Scientist*, 24 April 1986.)

Many of those who have looked after children with some of the diseases that embryo research is geared to prevent, agree:

> We know, personally and professionally, not only the tragedy of children dying of incurable diseases but the tragedy of lives limited by handicap. Modern medicine is on the brink of preventing conditions that lead to damaged lives or certain death, but this knowledge will be futile unless further research to develop healthy embryos is undertaken. (Brian Rix *et al*, *The Times*, 4 June 1985.)

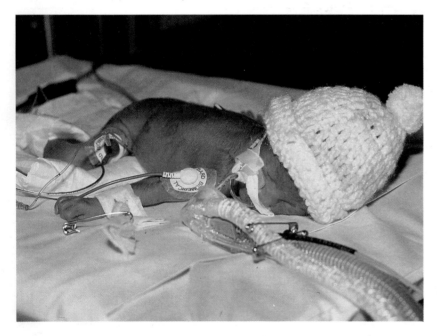

One of a set of triplets born as a result of in vitro fertilization. It is not uncommon for multiple pregnancies to arise from this treatment. However, this may cause problems, as the fetuses may be too small to survive, or they may be easily miscarried.

But others question our priorities:

> . . . we live in a society where perfection has become an entitlement. Everyone thinks they're entitled to a nice home, a nice car, a nice foreign holiday; everyone thinks they're entitled to perfect health, now science can deliver so much; everyone thinks they're entitled not only to children but to perfect children. Sometimes, however, the price is just too high. (Melanie Phillips, *Guardian*, 1 December 1989.)

To the anti-abortionists it is, quite simply, wrong to sacrifice some embryos for the good of others:

> We have no problem with therapeutic experimentation which will help a particular embryo to life and growth. What is immoral is using an embryo as a means to an end.
>
> We object to experimentation which kills the patient. We are saying that scientists should abide here by the same principles of medical ethics that apply to all other fields of medicine, where destructive research on human subjects is not allowed. (Sir Bernard Braine, *The Times*, 3 April 1990.)

It is ironic that infertile couples — who have struggled so hard to conceive — are now faced with the dilemma of whether their 'spare' embryos should be destroyed, not only in the laboratory but even after they have been replaced in the womb.

Putting five or six embryos back into the womb increases the chance of a pregnancy. But, if several embryos implant in the womb, there is a greater risk of miscarriage. So some women are being advised to have one or more embryos in the womb destroyed:

> For pregnancies with five or more fetuses, it is highly likely that all the fetuses will die, and triplet and quadruplet pregnancies also carry high perinatal [between the seventh month of pregnancy and the first week of life] mortality rates. Selective feticide is not, therefore, trading one life that could be saved for another. Indeed, in such cases it maximises the chance that any of the fetuses will survive.
>
> We believe that it is the best way in clinical practice to show respect for the substantial moral status of the fetus and whatever rights it may possess. (Dr R. J. Wapner et al, *Lancet*, 1990, vol 1, p 90.)

But the reality, for the woman whose instinct is to protect all the embryos, is very hard.

Some conditions that can be detected pre-natally

Spina bifida
Anencephaly
Down's syndrome
Cystic fibrosis
Some metabolic abnormalities
Many physical defects e.g: heart, lung and intestinal malformations

> The doctor explained that he would inject special salty water and that the needle would go into my tummy and . . . puncture the babies' hearts – they were going to do it like that. And the babies stay inside you – they don't come out or go rotten, they just stay there as tissue . . . And the worst part of it all is that they jumped. I felt it. I felt them moving. I felt them fighting. ('Frances', *Guardian*, 28 November 1989.)

Medical technology has also brought new dilemmas for women whose fetuses are found to be abnormal. Who is to decide the rights of these fetuses?

> It was already kicking inside me and was a person I felt I knew. But the disabilities which we were warned about left us in no doubt that we did not want to bring this person into the world . . .

>   We could have coped with some of the physical handicaps like a cleft palate, dropped jawline and the fact the baby would be floppy and not able to crawl or walk.

>   There were other indications though of disabilities connected with the liver, heart and kidneys which meant the child would suffer greatly . . . We felt we must take responsibility for our actions and not let somebody else do it for us. What we had to ask ourselves was could we cope? We had two other children under five so it was a difficult decision. (Johanna Kaufmann, *Sunday Express*, 12 November 1989.)

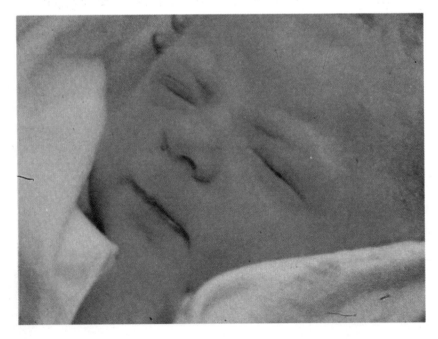

Louise Brown, the world's first test-tube baby. Who could have forecast that her birth should have led to so many ethical dilemmas for infertile couples.

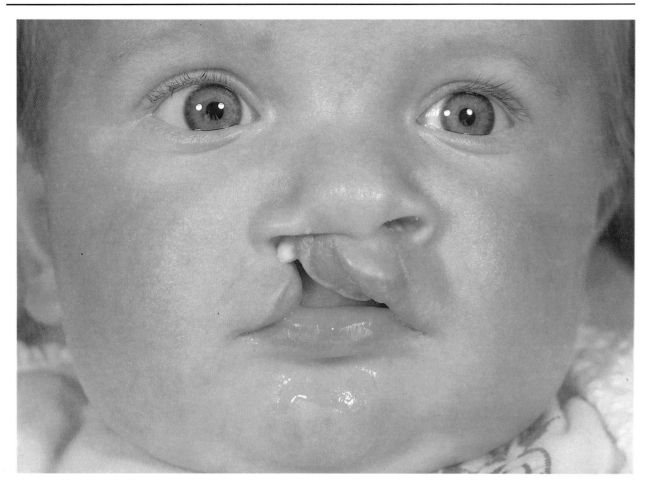

This child was born with a cleft palate – not a condition that if discovered in the womb, would currently merit an abortion. But how far should we go in allowing parents to choose whether or not to abort malformed babies, and who will decide what those guidelines should be?

However, some people who have experience of bringing up a handicapped child would still not contemplate the abortion of an abnormal fetus:

> If I hadn't already had one it would be an easier decision but I've had W and she is classed as handicapped. But she's lovely, she seems as normal as can be, so I couldn't have an abortion after W, but if I hadn't had her, my idea of being handicapped would be different. (Anonymous mother of handicapped child, *Journal of Medical Ethics*, 1983, vol 9, p 152.)

Nor do the dilemmas end with the abortion. Do these dead fetuses have rights or can they be seen simply as a convenient source of spare organs? The discovery that patients with the incurable, progressively disabling condition of Parkinson's disease may benefit from implants of fetal tissue has left doctors in doubt once again about where the ethical boundaries should lie.

The British Medical Association (BMA) has stated that:

> Tissue may be obtained only from dead foetuses resulting

from therapeutic or spontaneous abortion . . .

Transplantation activity must not interfere with the method of performing abortions, nor the timing of abortions, or influence the routine abortion procedure of the hospital in any way . . . (*Philosophy and Practice of Medical Ethics*, 1988.)

This sort of research inevitably raises the spectre — however far-fetched — of babies being conceived specifically for their organs. Once again, the BMA has ruled that:

> The generation or termination of a pregnancy solely to produce suitable material is unethical. There should be no link between the donor and recipient.

There must be no financial reward for the donation of foetal material or a foetus . . . (*Philosophy and Practice of Medical Ethics*, 1988.)

Thus, we have seen that any discussion of the rights of the fetus can no longer be limited solely to the pros and cons of abortion. There are many related issues to be considered and each step of progress that science takes brings with it ever more complex ethical problems.

1 Do you think that a ten-day-old pre-embryo should have the same rights as a 24-week fetus?

2 Should a 24-week fetus that has serious abnormalities have the same rights as a healthy fetus of the same age?

3 Read the quote from Melanie Phillips again. Do you think she is right? Have our expectations become so high that we underestimate disabled people?

Stages of development of the human fetus

Time	Name	Organs developed
Up to two weeks	Pre-embryo	None Cells divide and implant in wall of womb (approx day 10) Most of these cells form the 'life support' system for the pre-embryo eg: placenta, yolk sac
Day 15/16	Embryo	'Primitive streak' appears — a line of cells that will eventually form the fetus
Day 28	Embryo	A bulge can be seen where head will be; also a tail, and tiny buds where arms will grow
Week 6	Embryo	Discernible head and neck, visible heartbeat
Week 8	Embryo	Intestines formed, other organs in place
Week 9	Embryo	Sexual characteristics, eyes, nose and mouth have appeared
Week 12	Fetus	Most internal organs are working and heart can pump blood around body
Weeks 22-24	Fetus	Lungs become sufficiently 'elastic' to function very occasionally
Weeks 12-40	Fetus	Further growth and development

7

Contraception v abortion

Many of the people who find abortion unacceptable do allow that mechanical and hormonal methods of contraception are necessary and effective methods of family planning. Yet it is thought that the intra-uterine device (IUD) works not by preventing an egg from being fertilized, but by stopping the fertilized egg from implanting in the wall of the womb.

> Nowadays the biggest hazard in the way of the blastocyst [fertilized egg] in search of a home is the intrauterine device, falsely called an intrauterine contraceptive when it is no such thing . . .
>
> Clearly . . . IUD abortion . . . is, apart from the increased blood loss and perhaps some pain, completely non-traumatic [for the mother]. No theologians, bishops, pro-life groups, psychiatrists or jurors sit on the case of the IUD acceptor. (Germaine Greer, *Sex and Destiny – the Politics of Human Fertility,* 1984.)

Equally, the 'morning after' Pill, taken within three days after unprotected sexual intercourse, is aimed at preventing a fertilized egg from implanting in the wall of the womb, even though the woman does not know whether she is pregnant.

It could, therefore, be regarded as an abortifacient rather than a contraceptive and should, perhaps, be seen in the same light as the new generation of abortion-inducing drugs currently under development.

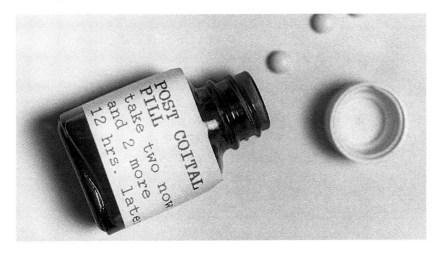

Thanks to the 'morning-after pill', thousands of women have never had to face the dilemma of whether to have their pregnancies terminated. Instead, the womb is made unwelcoming to any fertilized egg that may have passed through, and the woman need never know whether or not she had been pregnant.

Claude Evin (left), the French health minister who insisted that the abortion pill RU486 should go back on the market, so that women would have greater freedom of choice.

The best known of these is RU486 – a drug developed by a French pharmaceutical company – which induces abortion up to seven weeks of pregnancy. The outburst from French anti-abortionists led to the company withdrawing the drug from the market in October 1988, only for the French health minister to take the unprecedented step of insisting that it be reinstated:

> I could not permit the abortion debate to deprive women of a product that represents medical progress. I was doing what I could to make sure France did not surrender to pressure groups animated by archaic ideologies. (Claude Evin, French Health Minister, *New Statesman and Society*, 29 September 1989.)

Many doctors agree:

> How can we justify stifling research and development of a potentially simpler, safer and cheaper method of performing a procedure that is both legal and widespread in this country and others? Since we have granted women the right to make choices based on their own personal values, we must now go a step further and ensure a woman's maximum safety and well-being no matter which choice she makes.
>
> To permit social pressures to bridle [severely restrict] scientific inquiry is to cut ourselves off from needed advances in technology. (Diane Dahm, *Journal of the American Medical Association*, 1989, vol 262, p 1876.)

How RU486 works

RU486 is taken at the first stage of the abortion. It must be taken within the first seven weeks of pregnancy and it blocks hormone sites in the womb, making it hostile to the fetus. In the second stage, a different drug is given to soften the cervix and make it easier for the fetus to be expelled.

But anti-abortionists argue that drugs like RU486 will encourage women to see abortion as just another method of contraception instead of taking effective preventive measures:

> We want to see the abortion law tightened up in this country and this drug is going to make people think it's easy to have one. (Phyllis Bowman, Society for the Protection of the Unborn Child, *New Statesman and Society*, 29 September 1989.)

Once again, there is disagreement:

> There is simply no evidence that RU486 makes it easier to have an abortion or encourages women to have abortions. I see women seeking terminations and they do not do it lightly. It is an insult to say that women will use it as a form of contraception. (Professor David Baird, *Independent*, 15 August 1989.)

And some point out that even if we, in relatively well-off Western countries, can afford to miss out on RU486, others in the developing world cannot:

> This pill will save many lives in the third world where between 100,000 and 200,000 die every year as a result of abortions. (Professor Etienne-Emile Beaulieu, *General Practitioner*, 6 October 1989.)

Professor Etienne-Emile Beaulieu, whose research was crucial to the development of RU486.

Nevertheless, drugs like RU486 will revolutionize the abortion debate. Advances in the technology of pregnancy testing mean that a woman can already find out if she is pregnant, using a home testing kit, on the day her period is due — that is within two weeks of conception. A huge number of miscarriages occur naturally at this stage, generally without the woman being aware that she was pregnant. Because of this, it may be argued that aborting at this stage would have no greater physical or emotional consequences.

> . . . many of the products of conception are lost at varying stages of pregnancy. Of the eggs fertilised, up to half prove abnormal and are lost before the first week or ten days of pregnancy . . . (Malcolm Potts and Peter Shelman, *Society and Fertility*, 1979.)

There can be little doubt that most people do feel differently towards a fertilized egg only a few days old and a fetus which is recognizably human:

> . . . there is an obvious difference between the state interest in protecting the freshly fertilized egg and the state interest in protecting a 9-month, fully sentient [aware] fetus on the eve of birth. There can be no interest in protecting the newly fertilized egg from physical pain or mental anguish, because the capacity for such suffering does not yet exist; respecting a developed fetus, however, that interest is valid. (Justice John P. Stevens, *Daily Appellate Report*, 6 July 1989.)

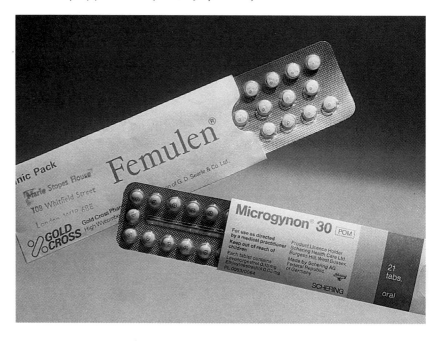

The combined hormonal Pill is the most effective form of contraception currently available. But scientists continue to look for better methods with fewer unwanted side-effects.

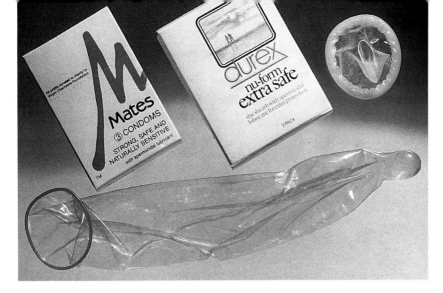

Condoms, if used correctly with water-based spermicidal lubrication, are not only highly effective contraceptives, they also protect against a wide range of sexually transmitted diseases, including AIDS.

So what is to stop early abortifacient drugs being used in a similar way to contraceptive pills? At present, use of RU486 is strictly limited to specialist clinics. However, it is not available in the UK; it is awaiting a product license following clinical trials and will not be in general use for several years. The manufacturers are determined that the drug will be carefully controlled:

> We want firstly to ensure that the drug's distribution channels throughout affiliated centres only and not through individual gynaecologists and the full administering process will be respected in all countries. We must also be careful the pill does not fall into the wrong hands. (Ariel Mouttet, *General Practitioner,* 6 October 1989.)

But what of the future? If a pill is developed that a woman can safely take on her own, should abortifacient drugs become more widely available, such as with a simple prescription from the family doctor on presentation of a positive pregnancy test? Not, it seems, in the USA, at least:

> An early abortion pill could provide a safer, less expensive, less painful, and more private and confidential alternative to the current surgical procedures. Yet there is little hope that American women will soon have legal access to RU486. No American drug company will go near it, even to conduct preliminary tests, because of pressure from anti-abortion groups, and the fear of protests and boycotts. Until such tests are done, the FDA [Food and Drug Administration] cannot approve the drug; and without that agency's approval no drug can be legally imported, manufactured or sold in the United States. (Mary Anne Warren, *Bioethics,* 1989, vol 4, p 320.)

1 Should abortifacient drugs be subject to stricter controls than contraceptives, or should they be available routinely to women in the first two months of pregnancy?

2 How would you feel about taking (or your partner taking) an abortifacient drug once a month instead of a contraceptive pill each day?

39

8

How doctors and nurses feel about abortion

Carrying out abortions is part of the everyday work of thousands of doctors and nurses all over the world. In many countries, doctors have promised, in their Hippocratic Oath, to do everything they can to save life:

> I will give no deadly medicine to anyone if asked, nor suggest any such counsel; and in like manner I will not give to a woman a pessary to produce abortion.

Some find it impossible to justify the need to take life:

> While the skilled pediatric surgeon is fighting for the life of the patient with congenital heart disease, the abortion clinic downstairs is turning a profit at the expense of countless, perfectly healthy first and second trimester [up to six months] fetuses. The hypocrisy is self evident . . . (J. Todd Williams, *Journal of the American Medical Association*, 1989, vol 262, p 1877.)

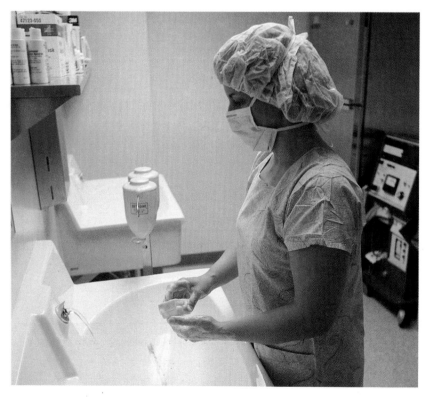

A nurse scrubs up, preparing to carry out an abortion. Some nurses do not agree with carrying out abortions, and refuse to do so.

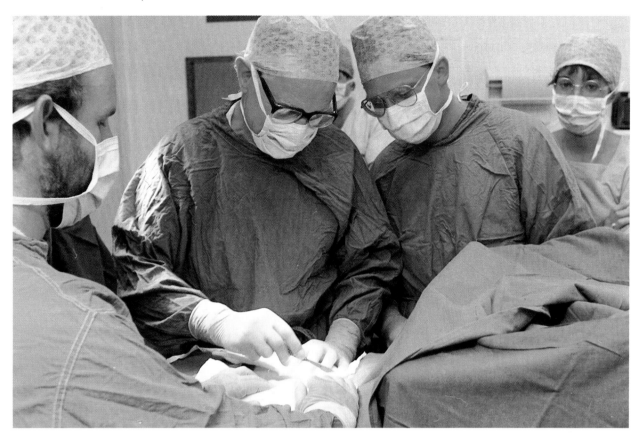

A life-saving operation in progress. From the cradle to the grave, everything possible is done by doctors and nurses to prolong life and improve its quality for their patients. Some doctors and nurses find it hard to accept abortion in comparison with this type of operation, while others feel that abortion is justified as an operation to improve the quality of life for the mother.

They also, it seems, make their views quite clear to the women seeking their help:

> What bothers me . . . is not so much the legal and financial aspects (stoicism and a grim sense of humour got me through) as the wilful denial of my human dignity and total lack of compassion and respect exhibited by the people on whom I had to rely for practical care. It has left me feeling abused, exploited and with the sense that out in the real world, becoming unintentionally pregnant outside wedlock still has 'stigma', 'scarlet woman' and 'silly little girl' written all over it. (Louise Minter, *Guardian*, 2 January 1989.)

Others are more sympathetic to the needs of the women:

> Late abortions — well, I wouldn't want to be in theatre [where operations take place] all the time. But, frankly, I feel more anguish listening to the women's stories. We had a late abortion last week, a widowed mother who'd found a man to love her after years alone. Then she found he was sexually abusing her children . . . (Nursing sister working at an abortion clinic, *Guardian*, 2 November 1989.)

In a recent survey of some 300 British gynaecologists, 73 per cent believed that women should have the right to choose whether or not to have an abortion. That would, in effect, make it easier to have an abortion, since, at present, in the UK, a woman must have the agreement of two doctors.

> Some have argued that right to choose would be unpopular amongst gynaecologists since they prefer to make the decision. The evidence from this study suggests that they are wrong . . .
>
> The time has come for British politicians to listen to the voice of the general public, backed by this new evidence that gynaecologists would support a liberalisation of the abortion law.
>
> (Wendy Savage and Colin Francome, *Lancet*, 1989, vol 2, p 1323.)

However, three-quarters of the gynaecologists surveyed wanted the time limit reduced from 28 to 24 weeks so that there would be fewer very late abortions. For it is these, as mentioned above, which are most distressing for medical staff. The fetus — perfectly formed — would, if resuscitated, stand a good chance of life.

A gynaecologist examining a woman's cervix. Gynaecologists see both the heartache of women who cannot cope with being pregnant and the joy of those who give birth to wanted children. It is up to them to be sure that each woman has all the information she needs to make this most difficult of decisions: whether or not to have an abortion.

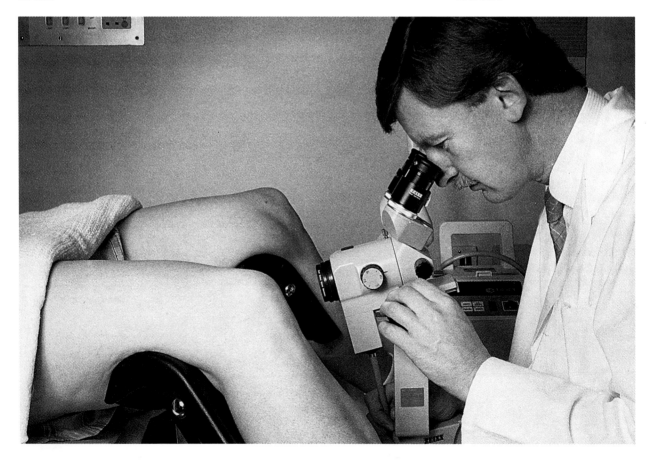

It has been suggested that, to save women the trauma of going into labour and giving birth to a fetus after the twelfth week of pregnancy, suction methods should be used to remove the fetus. However, at least one doctor has balked at such a suggestion since it would mean that the child would be dismembered in order to get it out:

> It is clear that physically dismembering and removing the fetus is emotionally distressing for the doctor. A doctor, therefore, has to overcome an element of revulsion in order to do a late surgical termination of pregnancy . . . dismemberment of the baby so violates a general human instinct that it is morally worse than destruction of the fetus by other means. (Richard Lilford and Nicholas Johnson, *Journal of Medical Ethics*, 1989, vol 15, p 82.)

But some believe that, whatever their own feelings, the woman's needs are paramount:

> The wellbeing of the woman who has made the painful decision to have her 20-week pregnancy terminated must be at the centre of the debate. The procedure must be the physically safest and least distressing possible . . .
>
> Dilatation and evacuation is distressing for the surgeon and for the theatre nurses but is much less distressing than medical abortion for ward staff and for other women who are patients in the ward. The distress felt in the theatre is acceptable if those involved are convinced that the abortion is necessary for the woman . . .
>
> Ideally the woman should make an informed choice of the method for her late abortion . . . (D. B. Paintin, *Lancet*, 1989, vol 2, p 563.)

It seems that, just as society in general has trouble deciding where the priorities should lie, so the members of the medical profession also find it hard to agree whether their duty is to their female patient or to some different moral code:

> Physicians have a high calling as advocates of life. Why do we too frequently refuse to extend this calling to include the unborn? Let us reevaluate the reality of abortion: the irreplaceable loss of all the dreams and possibilities contained within a unique life. Have we separated ourselves so far that we no longer recognize this for the tragedy that it is? (J. Todd Williams, *Journal of the American Medical Association*, 1989, vol 262, p 1877.)

Look again at the answers you gave to the questions at the end of chapter 2. Have any of your views changed through having read this book?

1   Under what circumstances do you believe abortion should be available?

2   Do you think it should be made harder or easier to get an abortion?

Conclusions

> My sorrow was immeasurable, penetrating every fibre of my being. I was wracked with sobs, heaving aching sobs, for an hour . . . After that day I spent three months plunged in total emotional darkness — the depths of anguish, anger and despair. I cried by day and by night for my lost baby. I wanted my child so desperately and could hardly come to terms with the fact that I had been directly responsible for my own child's death. (Anonymous woman, *Daily Mail*, 7 December 1989.)

A happy family enjoy one another's company. But some women choose abortion because they feel that they cannot give a child a good family life, either emotionally or financially.

Trying to decide whether or not to have an abortion is often one of the most difficult and distressing decisions of a woman's life.

Can anyone believe that a woman takes the decision lightly to abort her fetus? Even the radical feminist who tells us that nothing in the world matters except knowing she is not pregnant goes on to ask:

> Why then did both my abortions leave me bitter and angry in ways I could not, at that time, understand or explain . . . for me there seemed to be a contradiction between everything I had ever read or thought about abortion and the lived experience, an enormous gap between the impassioned rhetoric of the political and moral arguments both for and against abortion, and the bloody reality of one scared woman screaming on a table. (K. Kaufmann, *Test Tube Women*, 1984.)

The dilemma of abortion is not one that can be overcome by logical argument, by scientific fact or by emotional blackmail. Each case is different, each woman a person with her own needs, her own hopes and her own dreams. Who are we to judge her when she makes what must be the hardest decision of her life? And who is to say whether she was right or wrong?

Glossary

Abortifacient A drug that induces abortion, generally by making the womb reject the embryo.

Anencephaly A condition in which a fetus develops little or no brain. This will result in death at or within a few weeks of birth.

Blastocyst The developing fertilized egg, including surrounding membranes and tissues, between four and fourteen days after conception and generally up to 120 cells in size. When the embryo is at this stage of development, the woman is unlikely even to know she is pregnant.

Chromosome A thread-shaped structure in each cell that carries genetic information about all an individual's physical and mental characteristics. A human cell has 23 pairs of chromosomes and damage to one or more of these chromosomes can cause serious disease.

Conception Fertilization of a female egg by male sperm.

Cystic fibrosis A common, severe inherited disorder involving production of abnormal mucus throughout the body, especially in the lungs and intestines, leading to life-threatening tissue damage.

Down's syndrome A condition caused by a chromosome change, resulting in varying degrees of physical and mental handicap.

Embryo A developing mammal; in humans, this term is used up to the eighth week of pregnancy.

Fetus A developing mammal; in humans, this term is used from the eighth week of pregnancy until birth.

Gynaecologist A doctor who specializes in disorders of the female reproductive system.

Hippocratic oath The best known of the writings of the Greek physician Hippocrates, which sets out the moral code of ethics under which doctors practise.

Paediatrician A doctor who specializes in treating children's illnesses.

Perinatal The period from the seventh month of pregnancy up to the end of the first week of life.

Pre-embryo An alternative term to blastocyst, used by some embryologists to mean the fertilized egg and surrounding membranes up to the fourteenth day after pregnancy when the primitive streak appears.

Primitive streak A line of cells formed around the fourteenth day after fertilization, which will develop into the embryo.

Sepsis Infection.

Spina bifida A condition involving defective fetal development of the outside wall of the spinal canal, resulting in varying degrees of physical handicap and paralysis.

Further information

You can contact these organizations to find out more about the issues covered in this book.

Australia
Birthline, 20a Marlborough Street, College Park, South Australia 5069
Children by Choice, 237 Lutwyche Road, Windsor, Queensland, Australia 4030

Canada
Childbirth by Choice Trust, 344 Bloor Street West, Suite 306, Toronto, Ontario M5S 1W9
Right to Life Association of Toronto and Area, 144-A Yonge Street, Toronto, Ontario M5C 1X6

UK
British Pregnancy Advisory Service, Austy Manor, Wootton Wawen, Solihull, West Midlands B95 6BX
Brook Advisory Centre, 153a East Street, London SE17
Family Planning Association, 27-35 Mortimer Street, London WIN 7RJ
Life, 1a Newbold Terrace, Leamington Spa, Warwickshire CV32 4EA
National Abortion Campaign, Wesley House, 4 Wild Court, London WC2B 5AU
Pregnancy Advisory Service, 11-13 Charlotte Street, London SW1
The Society for the Protection of Unborn Children, 7 Tufton Street, London SW1P 3QN

Further reading

Charlish, Anne *Let's Discuss Abortion* (Wayland, 1989)
Law, Barbara *Contraception: Choice not Chance* (BMA Family Doctor Publications, 1986)
Saunders, Deborah *Let's Discuss Sex* (Wayland, 1987)
Trimmer, Eric *Knowing About Sex* (BMA Family Doctor Publications, 1986)

For teachers
Neustatter, Angela *Mixed Feelings* (Pluto, 1986)
Pipes, Mary *Understanding Abortion* (Women's Press, 1985)
Winn, Denise *Experiences of Abortion* (Macdonald Optima, 1988)

Picture acknowledgements

The publishers would like to thank the following for providing the illustrations in this book: Camera Press (Peter Abbey) 12, (Colin Davey) 19; Chapel Studios 6 (below); Mary Evans 7; Format (Jenny Matthews) 8, (Brenda Prince) 18, (Sue de Jong) 24, (Raissa Page) 25, (Maggie Murray) 35, 38, 39 & 42; Sally and Richard Greenhill 11, 14, 15; Network (Barry Lewis) 10; PHOTRI 4, 29, 40, 44, 45; Rex Features (Nils Jorgensen) 17, (SPG) 26 & 27, (Tom Wolmer) 30, 32, (Chamussy) 36, (Goyhenex) 37; Science Photo Library 21; St Mary's Hospital Medical School 33, 41; Topham 5, 16, 20, 23; Topham/TBS Colour Slides *cover*; UPP 13. The artwork on page 28 is by Jenny Hughes.

Index

Page numbers in **bold** refer to both illustrations and text. Others refer to text alone

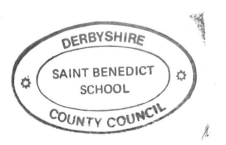